A PACEMAKER® CLASSIC

Helen Keller

The Story of My Life

Abridged and adapted by Amy Jolin
Illustrated by Angelo

GLOBE FEARON
Pearson Learning Group

Project Editor: David Cutts
Lead Editor: Amy Greenberg
Production Editor: Amy Benefiel
Marketing Manager: Kate Krimsky
Art Supervision: Angel Weyant, Eileen Peters
Art Coordinator: Cindy Talocci
Electronic Page Production: Leslie Greenberg, Susan Levine,
Wanda Rockwell
Manufacturing Supervisor: Mark Cirillo
Cover and Interior Illustrator: Angelo

ISBN: 0-130-23707-8
Printed in the United States of America

10 11 12 13 14   V036   15 14 13 12 11

1-800-321-3106
www.pearsonlearning.com

Contents

Major Characters

Helen Keller	The blind and deaf narrator
Kate Adams Keller	Her mother
Arthur H. Keller	Her father
Mildred Keller	Her younger sister
Martha Washington	Her childhood friend
Anne Mansfield Sullivan	Helen Keller's teacher
Mr. Anagnos	Principal of the Perkins Institution for the Blind
Mr. Gilman	Principal of the Cambridge School for Young Ladies
Dr. Alexander Graham Bell	Inventor who also promoted the cause of education for deaf people

1   Early Years

It is not easy to write the story of my life—my autobiography. When I think about my earliest memories, I almost forget what is true and what I have imagined. A few memories stand out from my first years. In this book, I shall try to write about only the interesting and important events.

I was born on June 27, 1880, in Tuscumbia, Alabama. One of my relatives, Casper Keller, came from Switzerland. His son was my grandfather, who settled in Alabama. My father was Arthur H. Keller. My mother, Kate Adams, was his second wife.

The first house I lived in had only two rooms. One was for my family. One was for the servant. The house was covered with vines and roses. The garden was full of flowers, and I knew it well. I knew all the smells. I also knew where the cool, shady spots were. Most of all, I knew where the roses were. They filled the whole air with their smell.

The beginning of my life was simple. I was the first baby in the family. My mother wanted to give me her mother's maiden name, Helen Everett. On the way to the church, my father forgot the name.

At the church, all he could think of was my grandmother's married name, Helen Adams. That is how I was named Helen Adams Keller.

When I was six months old, I could say "How d'ye." One day, I said "Tea, tea, tea" quite clearly. I also learned the word *water*. I would say "wah-wah." After my illness, I almost stopped speaking. "Wah-wah" was the one word that I kept using.

They say that I walked the day I was a year old. My mother had just taken me out of the bath. I saw the sunlight dancing on the smooth floor, and I almost ran to the light. Then, I fell and cried for her to pick me up again.

These happy days did not last long. When I was 18 months old, I became ill. My illness left me blind and deaf. The doctor thought I would not live. One day, however, my fever went away. My family was very happy. No one knew then that I would never see or hear again.

I have no clear memories of my illness. It seems like a bad dream. After my illness, I slowly got used to the silence and darkness around me. I almost forgot about lights and sounds. Then, my teacher came. She helped me to remember the sky, the trees, and the flowers that I had once seen.

I would sit in my mother's lap or follow her around the house. My hands felt every object. When I wanted something, I made up simple signs.

I shook my head to mean "No." A nod meant "Yes." A pull meant "Come." A push meant "Go."

At first, I did not know that I was different from other people. However, I knew it before my teacher came to me. I knew that my mother and my friends did not use signs. They talked with their mouths. Sometimes I stood between two people who were talking, and I touched their lips. I moved my lips and hands. They still could not understand me. This made me angry. Sometimes I kicked and screamed until I was tired.

In those days, I had a friend named Martha Washington. She was the cook's daughter. Martha understood my signs. We spent a lot of time in the kitchen. We kneaded dough balls and helped to make ice cream and grind coffee. We also fed the hens that came to the kitchen door.

One of the best games we played was to hunt for eggs in the grass. I could not tell Martha Washington when I wanted to go egg hunting. Instead, I would cup my hands and put them on the ground. This meant something round in the grass. Martha always understood. I never let her carry the eggs home. I thought that she might fall and break them.

One day, I spilled water on my apron and spread it out to dry by the fire. The apron did not dry quickly enough for me. I threw it right over the hot ashes.

The flames surrounded me, and my clothes caught fire. Luckily, my nurse heard me make a noise. She threw a blanket over me to put out the fire. Only my hands and hair were badly burned.

About this time, I found out how to use a key. One morning I locked my mother in the pantry and left her there for three hours. I could feel her pounding on the door. I thought that this was very funny. After that, my parents decided that they had to get a teacher for me. When my teacher, Miss Sullivan, came to me, I locked her in her room and hid the key. My father had to take Miss Sullivan out through the window. I thought that this, too, was very funny.

When I was five years old, we moved to a large new house. At that time, I had two older half-brothers. Later, my little sister, Mildred, was born. For a long time, I was jealous of my little sister. I would find her in my mother's lap. I knew that I was not the only child any more. One day, I found her in the cradle where I rocked my favorite doll. I was angry, so I rushed to the cradle and tipped it over. The baby might have been killed, but my mother caught her as she fell. Afterward, Mildred and I grew to love each other. She did not understand my signs. I did not understand her baby talk, but we played together happily.

2 Early Education

As the years passed, my desire to communicate grew. The few signs I knew became less and less useful. Most people did not understand me. This made me angry. I threw many tantrums. After these tantrums, I would cry until I was worn out. If my mother was near, I would creep into her arms. After a while, my outbursts happened every day. Sometimes they happened every hour.

My parents were worried. We lived far from any school for blind or deaf people. They were afraid no one would want to come to Tuscumbia to teach me. My friends and relatives sometimes wondered if I could be taught at all. My mother's only ray of hope came from a book she read. It was called *American Notes* by Charles Dickens. This book told the story of Laura Bridgman. Laura Bridgman was a blind and deaf girl who had been educated. Laura Bridgman's teacher was a man named Dr. Howe. He had discovered the way to teach deaf and blind children, but he had been dead many years. My mother was worried that his ideas had died with him.

When I was about six years old, my father heard of a famous eye doctor named Dr. Chisholm. My parents took me to Baltimore to see him. Perhaps he could do something for my eyes.

I remember the journey well. I made friends with many people on the train. One lady gave me a box of shells. My father made holes in them so that I could put them on a string. That kept me happy for a long time. The conductor was also kind. I often went with him on his rounds. He collected tickets and punched them. He let me curl up in a corner and use his punch to make holes in pieces of cardboard.

My aunt made me a big doll out of towels. It was a funny, shapeless thing. It had no nose, mouth, ears, or eyes. It bothered me that the doll had no eyes. I let everybody know that my doll needed eyes, but no one seemed able to fix the problem. Suddenly, I had a good idea. I tumbled onto the floor. I searched under the seat and found my aunt's cape. I pulled two beads off it and gave them to her. I showed her that they were to be sewn in the place for eyes. I could not contain my joy. With all the activity, I did not have one fit of temper.

When we arrived in Baltimore, Dr. Chisholm said he could do nothing for my eyes. However, he said that I could be educated. He told my father that he should talk to Dr. Alexander Graham Bell in Washington. Dr. Bell would be able to tell us about schools and teachers of deaf or blind children. We went to Washington right away. Dr. Bell was tender and kind. He held me on his knee and let me touch his watch. He made it strike for me. He understood my signs, and I knew it and loved him at once. I did not dream, however, that he would be able to help me to leave my darkness and find light. Through him, I would find friendship, knowledge, and love.

Dr. Bell advised my father to write to a man named Mr. Anagnos. He was the director of the Perkins Institution for the Blind in Boston. That was where Dr. Howe had worked with blind children. We were to ask for a teacher for me. My father did this at once. In a few weeks, we received a kind letter from Mr. Anagnos. He told us that a teacher had been found. This was in the summer of 1886.

The day my teacher came was the most important day of my life. Her name was Anne Mansfield Sullivan. It was March 3, 1887, and I was six years old.

On the afternoon of that day, I stood on the porch. There was a great hurrying in the house. That was how I could tell that something unusual was about to happen. I went to the door and waited on the steps.

Have you ever been on a boat in a dense fog? It seems as if a white darkness shuts you in. The boat can only feel its way toward the shore. I was like that ship before my teacher came. However, I did not know where the shore was. "Light! Give me light!" was the silent cry of my soul. My cry was answered in that very hour.

I felt footsteps coming near the house. I thought it was my mother. I stretched out my hand. Someone took my hand and gathered me in a great hug. This was my new teacher. She would show me many things. She would also grow to love me.

My teacher brought me a gift of a doll. The blind children at the Perkins Institution had made it. Laura Bridgman had dressed it. I did not know this until afterward. I began to play with the doll. After a little while, Miss Sullivan slowly spelled the word "d-o-l-l" into my hand. I was interested in this finger play. I tried to do the same thing. I was proud when I made the letters correctly. I ran downstairs to my mother and made the letters for *doll*. I did not know that I was spelling a word by using the manual alphabet. I did not even know that words existed. I was simply doing what my teacher did. In the next few days, I learned to spell many words. I learned *pin, hat,* and *cup*. I learned some verbs like *sit, stand,* and *walk*. However, it was several weeks before I understood that everything had a name.

One day, I was playing with my new doll. Miss Sullivan put my big rag doll into my lap also and spelled, "d-o-l-l." She tried to make me understand that "d-o-l-l" stood for both. Earlier in the day, we had worked on the words "m-u-g" and "w-a-t-e-r." Miss Sullivan had tried to explain that "m-u-g" is *mug* and that "w-a-t-e-r" is *water*. I kept getting them mixed up. She dropped the subject but later brought it up again. I grew impatient. I seized the new doll and threw it on the floor. I was delighted when I felt the pieces of the broken doll at my feet. I was not sad or sorry. I had not loved the doll. In my still, dark world, there was no tenderness. I felt my teacher sweep the pieces away. I was glad that the broken doll was gone. My teacher brought me my hat, and I knew I was going outside. This thought made me hop and skip with pleasure.

We walked down the path to the well-house. Someone was pumping water. My teacher placed my hand under the spout and cool water gushed over my hand. My teacher spelled the word *water* into my other hand. She spelled it slowly at first, then rapidly. I stood still. I was fixed on the motions of her fingers. Suddenly, I felt a faraway memory coming back to me. I felt a thrill of returning thought. Somehow, I discovered the mystery of language. I knew then that "w-a-t-e-r" meant what was flowing over my hand. That little word awoke my soul. That word brought me light, hope, and joy. I was set free!

I left the well-house eager to learn. Everything had a name, and each name brought a new thought. As we returned to the house, I saw everything with the strange, new sight that had come to me. When we entered the door, I remembered the doll I had broken. I felt my way to the pieces and tried to put them together. Then, my eyes filled with tears. I realized what I had done. For the first time, I felt sorry.

I learned many new words that day. I do not remember what they all were. I do know that I learned *mother, father, sister,* and *teacher.* The words made the world blossom for me. I was a happy child as I lay in my bed that night. I thought about the happy events of the day. For the first time, I looked forward to a new day.

After I learned language, I did nothing but explore with my hands. I learned the name of every object that I touched. I became happier with the rest of the world. When summer came, Miss Sullivan and I explored the fields. We went to the Tennessee River. We sat on the warm grass, and I had my first lesson in nature. I learned how the sun and the rain make things grow. I learned how birds build their nests. I saw how the animals find food and shelter. As I learned, I became delighted with the world. Miss Sullivan taught me to find beauty in the woods and in the world.

About this time, I had an experience that taught me that nature is not always kind. One day my teacher and I were returning from a long walk. The morning had been fine, but it was growing warm and steamy when we turned toward home. We stopped once or twice to rest under a tree. We stopped at last under a wild cherry tree near our house. The shade was good. I found the tree easy to climb. I scrambled to a seat in the tree with my teacher's help. It was so cool in the tree that Miss Sullivan thought we might have our lunch there. I promised to keep still while she went to get it.

Suddenly, a change passed over the tree. All the sun's warmth left the air. I knew the sky was black, because all the heat had died out of the air. I could smell the odor that comes before a thunderstorm. A fear clutched at my heart, and I felt absolutely alone. I was cut off from my friends and from the earth. I did not move, but terror crept over me. I longed for my teacher's return. Above all things, I wanted to get down from that tree.

Then, the leaves began to stir. A shiver ran through the tree. The wind sent a blast that almost knocked me off. I clung to the branch with all my might. The tree swayed and strained. Small twigs snapped and fell around me in showers. I wanted

to jump out of the tree, but I was too afraid to do it. I crouched down in the fork of the tree. The branches lashed around me. It felt as if something heavy had fallen. I was terrified. Just as I was thinking the tree and I would fall together, my teacher seized my hand. I clung to her. I trembled with joy to feel the earth under my feet once more. I had learned a new lesson. Nature is not always kind to her children.

After this experience, it was a long time before I climbed another tree. It was the sweet smell of the mimosa tree that finally made me get over my fear. One beautiful morning I was alone in the summer house reading. I smelled a lovely odor in the air. I started up and stretched out my hands. It seemed as if the spirit of spring had come. "What is it?" I asked. The next minute I recognized the smell of the blossoms.

I felt my way to the end of the garden. I knew that the mimosa tree was near the fence. Yes, there it was, quivering in the warm sunshine. Its branches almost touched the long grass. Was there ever anything so beautiful in the world? It seemed as if paradise had been brought to earth. I made my way through a shower of petals to the great trunk. For one minute I stood there. Then, I put my foot in the broad space between the forked branches and pulled myself up into the tree.

The bark hurt my hands, but I felt that I was doing something wonderful. I kept on climbing higher and higher. I reached a little seat that somebody had built in the tree, and sat there for a long, long time. I felt like a fairy on a rosy cloud. After that, I spent many happy hours in my little paradise. I thought lovely thoughts and dreamed bright dreams.

3 A Mind Awakens

Now that I had the key to all language, I was eager to learn to use it. Children who hear, learn language by hearing the words from people around them. The little deaf child learns words slowly and painfully, but the result is wonderful.

My teacher told me about many new things. At first, I asked very few questions, and my vocabulary was small. As I learned more and more words, I began to ask more questions. I would return again and again to the same subject. I was eager for more information.

I remember the morning that I first asked the meaning of the word *love*. I had found a few early violets in the garden. When I brought them to my teacher, she tried to kiss me. At that time, I did not like to have anyone kiss me except my mother. Miss Sullivan put her arm around me. She spelled into my hand, "I love Helen."

"What is love?" I asked.

She drew me closer and said, "It is here." She pointed to my heart. For the first time, I was aware of the beating of my heart. Yet, I was confused.

I could only understand the things I touched.

I smelled the violets in her hand, and asked, "Is love the sweetness of flowers?"

"No," said my teacher.

Again I thought. The warm sun was shining on us. I pointed in the direction of the heat and asked, "Is this not love?"

It seemed to me that there could be nothing more beautiful than the sun. However, Miss Sullivan shook her head. I was confused and disappointed. I thought it was strange that my teacher could not show me what love was.

A day or two later, I was stringing beads of different sizes. I would string two large beads, then three small ones. Miss Sullivan patiently pointed out my mistakes to me. Finally, I found a big mistake. I tried to think how I should have strung the beads. Miss Sullivan touched my forehead and spelled, "Think."

In a flash, I knew what *think* meant. It was the name of the process that was going on in my head. This was the first time I understood an idea.

For a long time, I was still. I was not thinking of the beads. I was trying to find a meaning for *love*. I pointed to the sun and asked my teacher again, "Is this not love?"

"Love is something like the clouds," she replied. Then, in simple words, she explained:

"You cannot touch the clouds, but you can feel the rain, and you know how glad the flowers are to have it on a hot day. You cannot touch love either. However, you can feel the sweetness that it pours into everything. Without love, you would not be happy or want to play."

The truth burst upon my mind. I suddenly felt as if I were somehow connected to others.

The process of learning language was long. It took many years. Deaf children do not learn language in a month or even in two or three years. Hearing children hear words all the time. The conversations they hear make them think. Soon, they are able to say what they think about things. This process is not possible for deaf children.

I could not hear the conversation around me, so my teacher tried to supply it. She did this by repeating what she heard and showing me how I could take part in the conversation. It was a long time before I could find the right things to say at the right times.

It is very difficult for deaf people and blind people to be good at conversation. It is even more difficult for people who are both deaf and blind! They cannot hear a person's tone of voice or see the expression on a person's face. They miss all the things that are not said in a conversation.

As soon as I could spell, my teacher wrote words on slips of cardboard. The words were written in raised letters. I learned that each printed word stood for something. I could arrange the words in little sentences. For example, I found the slips of cardboard that said "doll," "is," "on," and "bed." I put each name on its object. Then, I put my doll on the bed with the words *is, on, bed* beside the doll. In this way, I made a sentence with the objects themselves.

One day, I pinned the word *girl* on my dress and stood in the closet. I put the words *is, in, closet,* on the shelf next to me. My teacher and I played this game for hours at a time.

From the word slips, it was a short step to printed books. I had a book called *Reader for Beginners.* I would hunt for the words I knew. That was how I began to read.

For a long time, I had no regular lessons. Even when I studied hardest, it seemed more like a game than like work. Miss Sullivan explained everything as if she were a little girl herself. Studying with her is one of my favorite memories.

I do not know why Miss Sullivan was such a good teacher. She had been around blind children for many years, so she was very good at describing things. She would go quickly over boring details. She made every subject so real that I remembered everything she taught me.

Our favorite walk was to Keller's Landing. Keller's Landing was an old wharf on the Tennessee River. We spent many hours there learning about land and rivers. I built dams of pebbles. I made islands and lakes and rivers. I did not even know that I was learning a lesson. Miss Sullivan made raised maps out of clay. That way I could feel the mountains, valleys, and rivers with my fingers.

Arithmetic was the only study I did not like. I was never interested in numbers. Miss Sullivan had taught me to count by stringing beads in groups. I learned to add and subtract by arranging straws, but I had little patience. I could string only five or six groups at a time. I grew tired of it quickly and wanted to go out and play.

Miss Sullivan also taught me about animals and plants. One time, a man sent me a collection of fossils. They were shells and stones that held prints of a fern or a bird's claw. Miss Sullivan told me about the terrible beasts of long ago. For a long time, these creatures haunted my dreams.

I remember that we bought a lily to learn how plants grow. We set the lily in a sunny window. The slender leaves on the outside opened slowly. Soon the whole plant was covered with lovely flowers.

Once Miss Sullivan brought me 11 tadpoles in a glass globe. I remember feeling the tadpoles slip between my fingers. One day, one tadpole leaped out of the bowl. When I found it on the floor, it seemed almost dead. I put it back in the bowl, and it darted to the bottom and swam around. It had made its leap and had seen the great world. When it grew into a frog, it lived in a leafy pool at the end of the garden.

This was how my teacher taught me about life. She always pointed out the beauty in everything. She has made my life sweet and useful.

Any teacher can take children to the classroom. Not every teacher can make them learn. They will not work happily unless they feel that they do not have to. They must also feel success and failure for themselves.

The first Christmas after Miss Sullivan came was a great event. Everyone in the family made surprises for me. Miss Sullivan and I also made surprises for everyone else. I was thrilled with the mystery of the gifts. My friends tried to make me curious. They dropped hints about what they had for me. Every evening, Miss Sullivan and I tried to guess what the gifts would be. That guessing game taught me many things about language. I grew more excited as Christmas drew closer.

On Christmas Eve, the Tuscumbia schoolchildren invited me to visit their tree. It was loaded with lights and fruit. I danced around the tree happily. There was a gift for each child, and the teachers let me hand the gifts out. When I was ready for my gifts, I wanted to open them all—even the ones at home. I opened the ones from the schoolchildren right away. My teacher convinced me that it would be more fun to wait until morning for the others.

That night, I hung my stocking. I lay awake for a long time. I wanted to see what Santa Claus would do when he came. At last, I fell asleep. The next morning, I was the one who woke the whole family with my first "Merry Christmas!" I found surprises everywhere: They were on the table and on the chairs. They were at the door and on the window sills. I could hardly walk without stumbling on a bit of Christmas wrapped in paper. However, I was most happy with the gift from my teacher. She gave me a canary.

I named my canary Little Tim. It was so tame that it would hop on my finger. It ate candied cherries out of my hand. Miss Sullivan taught me to take care of my pet. Every morning, I made its bath and cleaned its cage. I filled its cup with fresh seed and water. I even hung a spray of chickweed in its swing.

One morning, I left the cage on the window-seat. I went to get water for its bath. When I came back, I felt a big cat brush past me. At first, I did not know what had happened. However, when I put my hand in the cage, Little Tim's pretty wings did not greet me. I knew that I would never see my sweet little canary again.

4 New Places

The next important event in my life was my visit to Boston in May 1888. I went with my teacher and my mother. This trip was not like the trip to Baltimore two years before. Then, I was a restless little girl. On this trip, I sat quietly beside Miss Sullivan. Miss Sullivan told me about what she saw through the window. She saw the Tennessee River and the great cotton fields. She saw the hills and the woods. She also told me about the people at the train stations who brought candy and popcorn balls through the train cars.

I took my big rag doll, Nancy. She sat on the seat across from me. She wore a new gingham dress and a ruffled bonnet. She looked at me out of two bead eyes. Mostly, I forgot about her. Sometimes, however, I remembered her and took her in my arms. I tried to believe that she was asleep and did not notice that I ignored her.

I will not mention Nancy again. However, I want to tell you about a sad experience that she had. She was covered with dirt—the remains of mud pies that I had made her eat. Someone from the laundry at the Perkins Institution took her and gave her a bath. This was too much for poor Nancy. When I saw her next, she was just a heap of cotton. I knew her only by the two bead eyes that looked at me angrily.

At last, the train pulled into Boston station. It was as if a fairy tale had come true. We went to the Perkins Institution for the Blind. I began to make friends with the little blind children right away. I could not believe that they knew the manual alphabet and could talk by using their fingers. It was wonderful to talk with other children in my own language!

I knew that I could not see, but it did not seem possible that my new friends were also blind. They could hear, so I thought that they must have a type of "second sight." When I talked, they felt my hand to listen. They read books with their fingers as well. I felt surprise and pain for them. However, they were so happy that I stopped feeling sorry and enjoyed their friendship.

While we were in Boston, we visited Bunker Hill. I learned about the brave men who had fought a battle on this spot during the American Revolution. I wondered if the soldiers had shot at the enemy from there.

The next day, we went to Plymouth by water. This was my first trip on the ocean. It was also my first time in a steamboat. It was full of life and motion! The rumble of the machinery made me think it was thunder, and I began to cry. I was afraid that if it rained, we would not be able to have our outdoor picnic. I was most interested in feeling the great rock where the Pilgrims landed. I was able to touch it, and that made the Pilgrims seem more real to me. I held a little model of Plymouth Rock in my hand and felt the numbers "1620" on it.

I thought the Pilgrims were brave to look for a new home in a strange land. I thought that they looked for freedom for themselves and for all men. Years later, I learned that they were not as freedom-loving as I had thought.

Among the many friends I made in Boston were Mr. William Endicott and his daughter. They were very kind to me. One day, we visited their beautiful home at Beverly Farms. I met their big dog, Leo, and their little dog, Fritz. Their horse, Nimrod, poked its nose into my hands for a lump of sugar. I also remember the beach there. For the first time, I played in the sand. It was hard, smooth sand. It was very different from the loose, sharp sand on the beach at Brewster. Mr. Endicott told me about the great ships that came sailing past. They were heading toward Europe. I saw him many times after that, and he was always a good friend to me.

We stayed at the Perkins Institution until the summer. Then, we made plans to spend our summer on Cape Cod with our friend, Mrs. Hopkins. I was excited. I had heard wonderful stories about the sea.

My most vivid memory of that summer is the ocean. I had never lived close to the sea. I had read about it in a big book called *Our World*. I wanted to touch the mighty sea and feel it roar.

As soon as we arrived, I got into my bathing suit and ran out to the warm sand. I did not think about being afraid. I plunged into the cool water and felt the great waves rise and fall. The motion of the water filled me with joy. Suddenly, my happiness turned to terror. My foot struck against a rock, and there was a rush of water over my head. I thrust out my hands to get some support. I clutched at the water and seaweed. The waves tossed me. It was frightening! At last, the sea threw me back on the shore. In another instant, my teacher's arms were around me. What a relief to feel her near! As soon as I had recovered from my panic, I asked: "Who put salt in the water?"

I soon recovered from my first experience in the water. I thought it was great fun to sit on a big rock and feel the waves dash against it. The spray covered me. I felt the pebbles rattle as the waves pounded the shore. The breakers swooped out and back. I clung to the rock and felt the roar of the rushing sea!

One day, Miss Sullivan showed me a strange object. She had captured a horseshoe crab in the shallow water. It was the first one I had ever seen. I thought it was very strange that it should carry its house on its back. I thought the crab might make a good pet. I took it by the tail with both hands and carried it home. We put the crab near the well where I was sure it would be safe. The next morning, it had disappeared! Nobody knew where it had gone. I was sad. Little by little, I came to realize that it was not kind to force this creature out of its home. I hoped that it had returned to the sea.

In the autumn, I returned to my home in Alabama. I spent the autumn months with my family at our summer cottage. The cottage was on a mountain about 14 miles from Tuscumbia. It was called Fern Quarry. It sat on the top of the mountain among oak and pine trees. Around the house was a wide porch. We ate and played on the porch most of the time.

Many visitors came to Fern Quarry. In the evening, the men sat by the campfire and told hunting stories. At night, the men slept in the hall outside our door. I could feel the deep breathing of the dogs. I felt the thumps the hunters made as they lay on their mats.

At dawn, I woke to the smell of coffee and the rattling of guns. The men made heavy footsteps as they stomped off to the hunt. Later in the morning, we started a barbecue. We lit a fire at the bottom of a deep hole in the ground and laid big sticks across the top. Then, we hung meat over the fire. The smell of the meat made me hungry long before the tables were set.

The days were exciting. We waited for the hunters to arrive. They were in good spirits, although they had not killed a single deer! They told stories about how close they had come. Soon, they forgot their disappointment. We sat down to a grand feast.

At the foot of the mountain, there was a railroad. About a mile away, there was a bridge for the train. It went over a deep valley. The bridge was very difficult to walk over. The railroad ties were wide apart. They were so narrow that they felt like knives under your shoes. I had never crossed it. One day Mildred, Miss Sullivan, and I were lost in the woods. We wandered for hours without finding a path.

Suddenly, Mildred pointed and said, "There's the bridge!" We would have taken any way rather than this. However, it was late and growing dark.

The bridge was a shortcut home. I had to feel for the rails with my toe, but I was not afraid. All at once there came a faint "puff, puff" from the distance.

"I see the train!" cried Mildred. In another minute, it would have been on us. We climbed down under the tracks while the train rushed over our heads. I felt the hot breath from the engine on my face. The smoke and ashes almost choked us. As the train rumbled by, the bridge shook and swayed. I thought we would fall to the valley below. With great difficulty, we climbed back on the track. Long after dark, we reached home, and the cottage was empty. Everyone was out looking for us.

Once I went on a visit to a New England village. I saw frozen lakes and big snow fields for the first time. I remember how surprised I was to discover that the trees and bushes were bare. The birds had flown away. Their empty nests were filled with snow. Winter was on every hill and field. The grass and bushes were a forest of icicles.

One day, we had a great snowstorm. We rushed outside to feel the first few tiny flakes. In the morning, all the roads were hidden. The land was a waste of snow with trees rising out of it.

In the evening, a wind from the northeast sprang up. The flakes rushed around madly. We sat around the great fire and told merry tales.

During the night, the wind made the roof creak and strain. The branches of the trees around the house beat against the windows with a clatter.

On the third day, the snowstorm ended. The sun came out and shone upon a white plain. Narrow paths were shoveled through the drifts. I put on my cloak and hood and went out. The cold air stung my cheeks like fire. We struggled to reach a pine grove. The trees stood motionless and white. There was no odor of pine needles at all. The rays of the sun fell upon the trees. The twigs sparkled like diamonds and dropped in showers when we touched them. The light was so dazzling that even I could sense its beauty.

As the days passed, the drifts gradually shrank. Before they were all gone, another storm came. I felt as though my feet did not touch the earth once all winter. Sometimes, the trees lost their icy covering and the bushes stayed bare. The lake, however, was frozen and hard beneath the sun.

Our favorite amusement during that winter was sliding down the slopes toward the frozen lake. We would get on our toboggan, and a boy would give us a shove. Off we went! We plunged through drifts and swooped down onto the lake. We would slide all the way across to the opposite bank. What joy! What exciting madness! For one wild moment, we joined hands with the winds. We felt divine!

5 The Dangers of Writing

It was in the spring of 1890 that I learned to speak. I had always wanted to make sounds with my voice. I would put one hand on my throat and feel it vibrate. With my other hand, I would feel my lips move. I liked anything that made a noise. To feel the cat purr and the dog bark made me happy. I also liked to put my hand on a singer's throat or on a piano when someone played it. Before I lost my sight and hearing, I had been learning to talk. After my illness, I stopped speaking because I could not hear. I used to sit on my mother's lap and keep my hands on her face to feel the motions of her lips. I moved my lips, too. However, I had forgotten what talking was. My friends say that I laughed and cried naturally. For a while, I made sounds just to exercise my voice. There was one word that I still remembered from before my illness: *water.* I pronounced it "wa-wa." This word became more and more slurred. I stopped using it after I had learned to spell the word on my fingers using the manual alphabet.

My thoughts would often come more quickly than my fingers could move. I kept using my lips and voice to help my fingers go faster. Some friends tried to discourage me from speaking. They did not want me to be disappointed. One day, I heard the story of Ragnhild Kaata. That was when I learned that a deaf child could learn to speak.

Ragnhild Kaata was a deaf and blind girl in Norway who had been taught to speak. I heard about her from Mrs. Lamson, who had been one of Laura Bridgman's teachers. When Mrs. Lamson finished describing Ragnhild Kaata's success, I became very eager to learn to speak. My teacher took me to Miss Sarah Fuller, principal of the Horace Mann School. Miss Fuller offered to teach me herself. We began lessons March 26, 1890.

Miss Fuller's method was simple. She passed my hand lightly over her face. She let me feel the position of her tongue and lips when she made a sound. I was eager to imitate her. In an hour, I had learned six sounds: *M, P, A, S, T, I.* Miss Fuller gave me 11 lessons in all. I will never forget the surprise and delight I felt when I said my first sentence: "It is warm." They were broken sounds, but it was speech.

Discovering speech was joyful for me. I began to talk to my toys, to stones, trees, birds, and animals. I was overjoyed when Mildred ran to me when

33

I called her and when my dogs obeyed my commands. It is wonderful to be able to speak in words that no one needs to interpret.

I had learned only the elements of speech. Miss Fuller and Miss Sullivan could understand me, but most people could not. I worked night and day before anyone could understand me. Miss Sullivan helped me to learn how the words were supposed to sound. Even now, she tells me every day about words that should sound better.

Teachers of deaf students know how hard it is to speak without hearing. I had to use the sense of touch to feel the vibrations of the throat. I would feel the movements of the mouth and the expression of the face. Often, my sense of touch was not correct. I had to repeat the words or sentences for hours. I tried to feel the proper ring in my own voice. My work was practice, practice, practice. Sometimes I became discouraged. The next moment, however, I remembered that I could show my family what I had learned. That made me keep working. I said to myself, "My little sister will understand me now."

It is much easier to talk than to spell with the fingers. As I got better at it, I almost completely stopped using the manual alphabet. Miss Sullivan and a few friends still use it to speak to me. It is faster than lip-reading.

I would like to explain how we use the manual alphabet. The person who talks to me spells with his or her hand by using single letters of the manual alphabet. These letters are the ones most deaf people use. I place my hands lightly over the speaker's hand. I can feel the letters as easily as a seeing person can see them. Constant practice makes the fingers very flexible. Some of my friends spell very rapidly—about as fast as an expert writing on a typewriter.

When I had learned to speak, I could not wait to go home. At last, the happy moment arrived. On the train home, I talked constantly with Miss Sullivan. I wanted to improve up to the last minute. Almost before I knew it, the train stopped at Tuscumbia station. My whole family stood there on the platform. My eyes fill with tears now as I think of it. My mother pressed me close to her. She was speechless and trembling with delight. Little Mildred took my free hand, kissed it, and danced. My father showed his pride in a big silence. It was a very happy meeting.

I must now tell about an unhappy time of my life that began in the winter of 1892. The root of my trouble was a little that story that I wrote. I sent it to Mr. Anagnos of the Perkins Institution for the Blind.

I wrote the story when I was at home during the autumn after I had learned to speak. We had stayed up at Fern Quarry later than usual. While we were there, Miss Sullivan had described to me the beautiful scenery. Her words brought back a memory of a story that must have been read to me as a child. At the time, I thought I was making up a story. I eagerly sat down to write it before I forgot it. My thoughts flowed easily. Words came quickly to my fingers, and I wrote each sentence on my slate. Today, I know that if words come to me that easily, they are probably not my own. At the time, though, I did not think about that. Even now, I cannot be sure if my ideas come from books or if they are my own.

When the story was finished, I read it to my teacher. I remember how happy I felt with it. At dinner, my teacher read it to my family. They were surprised that I could write so well. Someone asked if I had read it in a book.

This question surprised me very much. I did not remember that it was ever read to me. I spoke up and said, "Oh, no. It is my story. I have written it for Mr. Anagnos."

I copied the story and sent it to him for his birthday. Someone suggested that I change the title. I decided to change it from "Autumn Leaves" to "The Frost King." I carried the little story to the post office myself. I never imagined how sorry I would be for writing that birthday gift.

Mr. Anagnos was delighted with "The Frost King." He published it in one of the Perkins Institution reports. I could not have been happier. My happiness, however, did not last long. Someone discovered that there was a story similar to "The Frost King." It was called "The Frost Fairies," by Miss Margaret T. Canby. She wrote it before I was born in a book called *Birdie and His Friends*. The two stories were so much alike that Miss Canby's story must have been read to me as a child. My story used her words and ideas. That made my story a plagiarism, or a stolen story. I felt ashamed. I had embarrassed Mr. Anagnos. How could it have happened? I searched my brain for anything about the frost that I had read before. I could not remember anything except for reading about Jack Frost. I also remembered a children's poem called "The Freaks of the Frost," but I knew I had not used that in my story.

Mr. Anagnos was unhappy, but he seemed to believe me at first. To please him, I tried not to be unhappy. I tried to make myself as pretty as possible for a play we were giving for Washington's birthday.

The play was given by the blind girls. I remember that my costume had graceful folds. I wore autumn leaves around my head. I had fruit and grain at my feet and in my hands. I was excited about the play, but I had the feeling that something bad was coming.

The night before the play, one of the teachers asked me a question about "The Frost King." I told her that Miss Sullivan had talked to me about Jack Frost. She began to think that I remembered Miss Canby's story, "The Frost Fairies." She told Mr. Anagnos what she thought even though I told her she was mistaken.

Mr. Anagnos began to think that Miss Sullivan and I had tricked him. He thought that we tried to steal the thoughts of another writer to make him admire us.

He brought me in front of a court made up of teachers and officers of the school. Miss Sullivan had to leave me. They questioned me over and over. The teachers seemed to want me to admit that someone had read "The Frost Fairies" to me. I felt the doubt in every question. I also felt that Mr. Anagnos had begun to doubt me. The blood thumped in my heart. I could hardly speak. I knew that it was a mistake, but that did not make me less unhappy. When I was allowed to leave the room, my teacher was tender and kind. My friends said that I was a brave little girl and that they were proud of me.

That night in bed, I cried. I felt so cold that I hoped I would die before morning. However, I was young, and I have forgotten most of the horrible misery I felt then.

Miss Sullivan had never heard of the story "The Frost Fairies" or the book it was in. She found out later that Mrs. Sophia C. Hopkins had a copy of Miss Canby's book *Birdie and His Friends.* In 1888, we had spent the summer with her at Brewster. Mrs. Hopkins could not find her copy of the book. She told me that she remembered trying to amuse me while Miss Sullivan was on vacation. She read from several books. She could not remember reading "The Frost Fairies." However, she was sure that *Birdie and His Friends* was one of the books she read.

I did not understand the stories that Mrs. Hopkins read to me then. It was just a game to me. I must have tried to remember all of the words she spelled. I wanted to ask my teacher about them. The words must have been stamped on my brain. However, for a long time, no one knew it—not even me.

I did not talk to Miss Sullivan about the story when she came back. That was probably because she started to read other books to me. However, it is true that Miss Canby's story was read to me once. I had forgotten it for a long time. Nevertheless, it came back to me completely. I never dreamed that it was someone else's story.

In my trouble, I received many messages of love and sympathy. All the people I loved best are still my friends except one—Mr. Anagnos. Miss Canby even wrote kind words to me: "Some day you will write a great story of your own. It will be a comfort and a help to many."

I have never played with words again as a game. I have always been afraid that what I write is not my own. For a long time, when I wrote a letter, I was afraid. I would spell the sentences over and over to make sure I had not read them in a book. Miss Sullivan encouraged me. She did not want me to give up writing completely.

Since that time, I have read "The Frost Fairies." I also read the letters I wrote around that time. I saw that I used other ideas from the story. I even found a letter to Mr. Anagnos. I wrote it when I was writing "The Frost King." I found words exactly like those in the book. This letter shows that my mind was filled with the story.

In many of my early letters, I took words from my reading. Once, I wrote about the old cities of Greece and Italy. I borrowed my words from books. I knew Mr. Anagnos loved Italy and Greece, so I gathered all the beautiful things that I thought he would like. Mr. Anagnos liked my work about Italy and Greece very much. I do not understand how he ever thought a blind and deaf child of 11 could have made everything up. I believe that my little story is interesting even if it is borrowed. It shows me that I could express beautiful ideas in clear language.

Those early stories were exercises for my mind. I was a child learning to write. Like any other child, I imitated what I read. I put my ideas into words. I kept everything I read in my memory. I did not always mean to, but I did. I am afraid that I still do this. I hope to outgrow my borrowed stories someday. Perhaps, then, my own thoughts will come out in my writing. Until then, I try not to let the bad memory of "The Frost King" ruin my writing.

This sad experience may have done me good. It made me think about some of the problems of writing. My only regret is that I lost my dear friend Mr. Anagnos.

This has been my account of "The Frost King" experience. It was important in my life and education. I have given the facts as they appear to me. I do not mean to defend myself or to lay blame on anyone.

6 Preparing for College

I spent the summer and winter after writing "The Frost King" with my family in Alabama. It was good to go home. All of the flowers were out. I was happy. I had forgotten "The Frost King."

In the autumn, red and golden leaves covered the ground. The grapes in the garden turned golden brown in the sunshine. I began to write a record of my life. It had been a year since I had written "The Frost King."

I was still very worried about everything I wrote. I was afraid that my words might not be my own. Only my teacher knew about these fears. I never talked about "The Frost King." Sometimes, an idea flashed out in conversation. I would spell softly to her, "I am not sure it is mine." It would also happen when I was writing. In the middle of a paragraph, I would worry and say to myself: "Suppose all this was written long ago by someone else!" A fear would clutch my hand. I could not write any more that day. Even now, I sometimes feel the same fear. Miss Sullivan helped me in every way, but the terrible experience had left a lasting memory. I am only just beginning to understand it. Miss Sullivan tried to help me stop worrying by asking me to write a story of my life for a magazine. I was 12 years old at that time. It was hard to write that little story. I must have known that something would come out of it. Otherwise, I would surely have failed.

I wrote timidly and fearfully. My teacher urged me on. She knew that I would soon find my way again and get a grip on my mind. Before "The Frost King" experience, I had been a little child. Now, my thoughts were turned inward. I had begun to grow up. Gradually, my mind began to clear. I had begun to learn a little bit about life.

The year 1893 was busy. I took a trip to Washington and saw Mr. Grover Cleveland sworn in as president. I also visited Niagara Falls and the World's Fair. All of these trips broke up my studies, which were sometimes delayed for weeks.

We went to Niagara Falls in March 1893. I stood on the point that overhangs the American Falls. I felt the air vibrate around me and felt the earth tremble.

Many people wonder why I loved Niagara. They cannot understand how I could feel the beauty. They ask me, "What does this beauty or that music mean to you? You cannot see the waves rolling up the beach or hear their roar. What do they mean to you?" These things mean everything to me!

I cannot explain it. It is as hard to explain as love or religion or goodness.

Miss Sullivan and I visited the World's Fair during the summer of 1893. We went with Dr. Alexander Graham Bell. I remember how thrilled I was. Every day in my imagination I made a trip around the world. I saw many wonders from the farthest parts of the earth. I saw great new inventions and machines. The entire world seemed to pass under my fingertips.

Each booth was full of interesting things. I saw the India of my books. There was a model of the Pyramids with a long string of camels. In another area, I saw the canals of Venice. We sailed there every evening when the city was lit. I also went on a Viking ship and saw how the seamen sailed their ship. They had strong arms and steady hearts.

A little way from this ship there was a model of the *Santa Maria*. The captain of this ship showed me Columbus's cabin. I saw his desk. It had an hourglass on it. I imagined Columbus watching the sand drop grain by grain. He must have felt very tired.

Mr. Higinbotham was president of the World's Fair. He kindly let me touch the exhibits. I was able to see the glories of the fair with my fingers. I learned many things. At the Cape of Good Hope exhibit, for example, I learned about mining diamonds. I was able to touch the machines while

45

they were in motion. That way, I got to learn how the stones were weighed. I could tell how they were cut and polished. I searched in the water for a diamond. I found one myself.

Dr. Bell went everywhere with us and described to me the things he saw. In the electrical building, we examined telephones and other inventions. He made me understand how to send a message on wires. In other exhibits, I saw the ruins of ancient Mexico, old stone tools, and mummies. I remember that I did not want to touch the mummies.

All these experiences added new words to my vocabulary. In the three weeks I spent at the fair, I took a long leap from fairy tales and toys to an appreciation of the real things in the world.

At the end of that summer, I began my studies again. I read the histories of Greece, Rome, and the United States. I also studied a French grammar text in raised print. I enjoyed French. I tried writing short exercises in my head using the new words. I ignored rules as much as possible. I even tried to speak French using all the letters and sounds that were described in the book. Of course, this was a very difficult task.

I also worked to improve my speech. I read my favorite poetry aloud. Miss Sullivan listened. She corrected me and helped me to pronounce each word correctly. By October 1893, I began to have regular lessons. Each day I would have lessons at fixed hours.

Miss Sullivan and I were in Hulton, Pennsylvania at that time. We were visiting the family of Mr. William Wade. Mr. Wade's neighbor, Mr. Irons, was a good Latin teacher. I began to study with him. He taught me mostly Latin grammar, but he also helped me in math. I found math difficult and uninteresting. I was much more interested in poetry. Mr. Irons had me read the poem "In Memoriam" by Tennyson from a critical point of view. This was new to me. Mr. Irons helped me to understand it. He helped me recognize an author's style as I would recognize a friend's handshake.

At first, I did not want to study Latin grammar. I did not want to examine every word. When I got deeper into the subject, I became more interested. Miss Sullivan sat beside me at my lessons. She spelled into my hand whatever Mr. Irons said. She also looked up new words for me. I began to think the language was beautiful, and I sometimes read passages just for fun. I picked up words I understood and tried to make sense of them. This is a hobby that I still enjoy.

In the summer of 1894, I attended a meeting about teaching speech to deaf people. At that meeting, arrangements were made for me to go to the Wright-Humanson School for the Deaf in

New York City. I went there in October 1894 with Miss Sullivan. We chose this school because I could learn speaking and lip-reading there. During my two years at the school, I also studied math, geography, French, and German.

Miss Reamy, my German teacher, could use the manual alphabet. After I learned a few words in her language, we could talk together in German. In a few months, I could understand almost everything she said. I did better in German than in any other class. French was more difficult. I studied it with Madame Olivier—a French lady who did not know the manual alphabet. She taught her class by speaking. I could not read her lips easily. Therefore, my progress was much slower than in German.

My progress in lip-reading and speech was not what my teachers and I had hoped it would be. I wanted to speak like other people. My teachers believed that this could be done. We worked hard, but we did not quite reach our goal. I suppose we aimed too high. We were disappointed.

I was also disappointed in my math studies. I thought math was a system of pitfalls. The main trouble was that I tried to guess the answers to the problems. I did not want to work them out.

I studied eagerly in my other subjects. I especially liked geography. It was a joy to learn the secrets of nature. I learned how the winds blow, how the clouds are made, how rivers cut through rock, and how mountains are turned up. The two years in New York were happy ones. I look back to them with real pleasure.

I remember especially the walks we took in Central Park. The park was the only part of the city that was friendly to me. Miss Sullivan would describe it to me every day. It was beautiful and different each day!

In the spring, we took trips to interesting places. We sailed on the Hudson River. I liked the grand cliffs along its banks. We also visited West Point and Tarrytown, the home of Washington Irving.

The teachers at the Wright-Humanson School tried to help the students live like hearing children do. They tried to lead us out of our usual surroundings.

7 The Cambridge School

In October 1896, I began to study for college. I went to the Cambridge School for Young Ladies. I was getting ready to go to Radcliffe, an all-girls college in Cambridge, Massachusetts.

When I was a little girl, I visited a college for girls in Massachusetts called Wellesley. I told my friends, "Some day I will go to college—but I will go to Harvard University!" They were surprised. When asked why I would not go to Wellesley, I replied that there were only girls there. Going to college became fixed in my mind. Soon it was my most precious dream. I wanted to study with seeing and hearing girls. Many of my friends thought this idea was impossible. When I left New York, I decided to keep studying for college. I would go to Cambridge. This was as close as I could get to Harvard and to my dream of going to college.

At the Cambridge School, Miss Sullivan attended classes with me. She spelled the words the teachers said.

Of course, my teachers had never taught a blind and deaf student. I could only "hear" them by reading their lips. My studies for the first year were English history, English literature, German, math, and Latin. Until then, I had never studied with the idea of preparing for college. I had been well drilled in English by Miss Sullivan. My teachers saw that I did not need special help in this subject. I had a good start in French. I had studied Latin for six months. I was most familiar, however, with German.

There were drawbacks to my progress. Miss Sullivan could not spell out every word from every book. Also, it was very hard to have the textbooks set in raised print in time for class. My friends in London and Philadelphia, however, worked hard to get them to me quickly. For a while, I had to copy my Latin in Braille so that I could learn with the other girls. My teachers soon began to understand my imperfect speech. They could answer my questions and correct mistakes. I could not make notes in class or write exercises. I wrote all my papers at home on my typewriter.

Each day, Miss Sullivan went to the classes with me. She patiently spelled into my hand all that the teachers said. In study hours, she had to look up new words for me. She read the notes and books that I did not have in raised print. This work was very tiring for her. Only two teachers learned the manual alphabet. One was Frau Gröte, my German teacher. The other was Mr. Gilman, the principal.

Frau Gröte's spelling was very slow, and she knew it. However, she was a good person because she spelled out her lessons to me twice a week. That gave Miss Sullivan a little rest. Everybody was kind and ready to help us. However, Miss Sullivan was the only person who could turn hard work into fun.

That year, I finished studying math. I reviewed my Latin grammar and read three chapters of Caesar's *Gallic War*. I also read many German books. Some of these I read with my fingers. Others I read with Miss Sullivan's help.

Mr. Gilman was my English teacher. We read a play and several histories together. He made my work easy. He explained things in clever ways. I enjoyed studying with him.

At the Cambridge School, I got to know seeing and hearing girls of my own age. This had never happened before. I lived with several girls in a pleasant house connected to the school. We all enjoyed a homey life. I joined them in many of their games—even blindman's bluff. I took long walks with them. We talked about our studies, and we read aloud the things that interested us. Some of the girls learned to speak to me. As a result, Miss Sullivan did not have to repeat their conversation.

At Christmas, my mother and little sister came to visit me. Mr. Gilman kindly offered to let Mildred study in his school. So Mildred stayed with me in Cambridge. We were together for six months. It made me very happy to study and play with her.

I took the early examinations for Radcliffe between June 29 and July 3, 1897. There were five subjects. They were German, French, Latin, English, and history. I passed every exam. I did very well in German and English.

I think I should explain how I took my tests. I had to take a total of 16 hours of tests. Twelve hours were for elementary tests. Four hours were for advanced tests. I had to pass five hours at a time to have them counted. The tests were given out at nine o'clock in the morning at Harvard. A special messenger brought them to Radcliffe. Each student was given a different number. We wrote our numbers on our test papers. We did not write our names. This way, no one could easily tell who wrote which test. I was Number 233. However, I was the only student using a typewriter. The teachers knew which paper was mine. They did not need to see my number.

My teachers decided that I should take my exams in a room by myself. They thought the sound of the typewriter might bother the other girls. Mr. Gilman read all of the papers to me. He used the manual alphabet. A man was placed on guard at the door to make sure that no one bothered me.

The first day I had German. Mr. Gilman sat beside me and read the paper through first. Then, he read it again sentence by sentence. I repeated the words aloud to be sure that I understood him perfectly. The papers were difficult. I felt very nervous as I wrote out my answers on the typewriter. Mr. Gilman spelled to me what I had written. I made any needed changes, and he inserted them into my paper. This has never happened on any other test. At Radcliffe, no one reads the papers to me after they are written. I have no chance to correct any errors. Sometimes, I finish before the time is up. In that case, I try to remember what I have written. I try to correct the mistakes and write the corrections at the end of my paper.

I did well on these early tests—better than on the final tests. There are two reasons for this. In the finals, no one read my work over to me. Also, the early tests were on subjects that I knew well. I had already passed practice exams in English, history, French, and German, which Mr. Gilman had given me at the beginning of the year.

After each test, Mr. Gilman sent my work to be graded.

I took all the other tests in the same way. None of them was as difficult as the first one. I remember the day the Latin paper was brought to us.

Professor Schilling came in and told me I had passed my German test. This encouraged me greatly. I sped on to the end of the Latin test with a light heart and a steady hand.

I was full of hope when I began my second year at Mr. Gilman's school. During the first few weeks, I faced some problems. Mr. Gilman had agreed that I should study mostly math. I was also going to study physics, algebra, geometry, astronomy, Greek, and Latin. Many of the books I needed were not ready when I began classes. The classes I was in were very large, and the teachers were not able to give me special help. Miss Sullivan had to read all the books to me and interpret for the teachers.

Geometry and physics were the most difficult for me. It was hard for me to figure out problems in class. I needed a Braille writer to do this. With a writer, I could type out the problem. I would be able to read it myself. I could also put down the steps to figure it out. That way, I would not have to remember all my work.

In geometry, I could not see the figures on the blackboard. To get a clear idea of them, I tried making each figure on a cushion using straight and curved wires with bent and pointed ends. I had to try to remember the letters of each figure. Then, I would work to figure out the problem.

In short, every study was difficult in its own way. Sometimes, I became discouraged. I am ashamed to recall the way I behaved—especially since my troubles were later used against Miss Sullivan. She was truly the only person who could make problems disappear.

Little by little, my problems were solved. The books that I needed arrived. I began working very hard. I was sure I would succeed. Algebra and geometry were the only studies that continued to give me trouble. As I have said before, I am not good at math. Geometry was a special problem because I could not see the diagrams. I could not tell how each part related to the others. Even my cushion did not help with this. I struggled for a long time. I only began to understand math when Mr. Keith taught me.

I was beginning to get past all these difficulties. Then, everything changed.

Just before my books came, Mr. Gilman told Miss Sullivan that he thought I was working too hard. He had decided that I should take fewer classes. From the beginning, I had planned to take up to five years to prepare for college. However, I did well in my first year. I had passed all of my tests. Miss Sullivan and Miss Harbaugh (Mr. Gilman's head teacher) were very happy. They agreed that I might finish in only two more years.

Mr. Gilman agreed to this at first. Now, he thought I was working too hard. He decided that I should stay at his school three years longer. I did not like his plan. I wanted to enter college with my class.

On November 17, I was not well and did not go to school. Miss Sullivan knew that I was not seriously sick. Yet, Mr. Gilman heard of it and said that I was breaking down. He made changes in my studies. The changes meant that I could not take final exams with my class. In the end, Mr. Gilman and Miss Sullivan disagreed. My mother was unhappy. She decided to withdraw my sister, Mildred, and me from the Cambridge School.

We decided that I would continue my studies with a tutor. He was Mr. Merton S. Keith, from Cambridge. Miss Sullivan and I spent the rest of the winter with our friends, the Chamberlins. They lived in Wrentham, 25 miles from Boston.

I studied with Mr. Keith from February to July 1898. He came out to Wrentham twice a week, and taught me algebra, geometry, Greek, and Latin. Miss Sullivan interpreted his words for me.

We returned to Boston in October 1898 and lived there for the next eight months. Mr. Keith gave me lessons five times a week. Each lesson lasted for about an hour. He explained the things I did not understand, and he assigned new work. He also took home the Greek exercises that I had written during the week. He corrected them and returned them to me the next week.

This was how I studied for college. It was much easier to be taught by myself than in a class. There was no hurry or confusion. My tutor had plenty of time to explain new information. As a result, I learned faster. I also did better work than I ever did in school. Mr. Keith made math problems small enough for me to understand. He kept my mind alert and eager. He taught me to think clearly. He helped me be calm and logical and did not let me guess the answers.

On June 29 and 30, 1899, I took my final exams for Radcliffe. The first day, I had elementary Greek and advanced Latin. The second day, I had geometry, algebra, and advanced Greek.

The college did not allow Miss Sullivan to read the test papers to me. Instead, Mr. Eugene C. Vining, a teacher from the Perkins Institution for the Blind, was hired. Mr. Vining copied the papers into American Braille. I did not know Mr. Vining. He did not try to speak to me in any way.

I could easily read the Braille on the language tests. It was not so easy, however, for geometry and algebra. I was confused and felt discouraged. I wasted time trying to read the tests. I know all three types of Braille: English, American, and New York Point. However, the symbols in the three systems are very different. I did not know all the math symbols. I had used only the English Braille symbols in my algebra.

The algebra test was in American Braille. Only two days before the test, Mr. Vining sent me a Braille copy of an old Harvard test. I was very worried. I wrote to Mr. Vining right away and asked him to explain the signs. He sent back another paper and a table of signs. I tried to learn the symbols quickly. I worked late on the night before the algebra test. I was struggling over some very difficult problems. I could not understand the combinations of symbols. Both Mr. Keith and I were worried. We went to the college before the test began. Mr. Vining then explained the American symbols better.

I took the geometry test first. It was very hard. I had always read the problems in line print or had them spelled into my hand. On the test, I found the Braille confusing. The problems were not what I was used to. I could not figure out what I was reading. Then, I started algebra. This test was even harder. Mr. Keith had let me solve problems in my mind. He had not taught me to take tests. Therefore, my work was painfully slow. I had to read the examples over and over before I could tell what I was supposed to do. I found it very hard to keep my wits about me.

I do not blame anyone. The teachers at Radcliffe did not realize how difficult they were making my tests for me. They did not understand my difficulties. However, I did well on my tests. I am proud of my work. My difficulties did not stop me from going to college.

8   **Radcliffe**

The tests to get into college had been difficult. I could now enter Radcliffe whenever I wanted. We decided, however, that I should study for one more year with Mr. Keith. Therefore, it was not until the fall of 1900 that my dream of going to college came true.

I remember my first day at Radcliffe. It was a wonderful day for me. I had looked forward to it for years. A force inside me had driven me to test myself next to people who could see and hear. I knew that there would be problems in the way, but I looked forward to solving them.

I began my studies eagerly. I saw a new world opening, and I was sure I could learn all things. In my mind, I was as free as any other girl. The lecture halls seemed filled with greatness. I thought that the professors were wise. If I have since learned that it is not true, I am not going to tell anybody.

Soon I discovered that college was not the wonderland I thought it would be. My childish dreams faded. Going to college would not be easy.

I found that one very big problem at college was that I never had enough time. There is no place for dreams or imagination. College is a place to learn— not to think about things.

I studied four subjects my first year. They were French, German, history, and English.

People often ask how I could work the way I did in college. In the classroom, I am, of course, almost alone. The professor is far away. Miss Sullivan spells the lectures into my hand as quickly as possible. I lose much because we go so fast. The words rush through my hands like hounds chasing a rabbit. I do not think I am much worse off than the girls who take notes are. They are trying to write words on paper just as fast. I cannot write notes during the lecture. My hands are too busy listening. I try to remember what I hear and jot down some notes when I get home. I write the homework on my typewriter. That way, the professors have no difficulty in finding out how little I know.

I use the Hammond typewriter. I have tried many machines, but I find the Hammond is the best for me. It has movable type shuttles, and each shuttle has a different set of letters. A shuttle can be Greek, French, or mathematical. I choose the shuttle I need for each subject. I doubt if I could go to college without this typewriter.

Very few of the books I need are printed for the blind. I have to have them spelled into my hand. Therefore, I need more time to prepare for each lesson than the other girls do. There are days when the many details make me feel sorry for myself. I know that other girls are laughing and singing and dancing, but I must spend hours reading a few chapters. This makes me angry, but soon I laugh at myself. After all, everyone who wishes to gain true knowledge has difficulties. There is no easy path to success. I must make my own way. I slip back many times. I lose my temper and find it again. I plod on. I gain a little. I feel encouraged. Every struggle is a victory. I am not always alone, however, in these struggles. Mr. William Wade and Mr. E. E. Allen, principal of the Pennsylvania Institution for the Instruction of the Blind, are with me. They get many of the books I need in raised print. Their work has helped me more than they can ever know.

Last year was my second year at Radcliffe. I studied English, the Bible as literature, American government, and Latin. The class in English was my favorite. It was very lively. The lectures were always interesting and funny. The teacher was Mr. Charles Townsend Copeland. He made each book fresh and powerful, and he taught me to love all the classic books and listen to the authors' fine thoughts.

I enjoyed the sweet thunder of the Bible. I went home feeling that I had touched something perfect.

This year is the happiest because I am studying subjects that really interest me. I am taking economics, English, Shakespeare, and philosophy.

College, however, is not the perfect world I thought it would be. I have not met great and wise writers face to face. I do not even feel their living touch. They are there, but they seem like mummies. We must read them carefully before we can be sure that they are truly great and wise.

I do not object to reading the famous works. I only object to endless criticisms that teach only one thing. There are as many opinions about books as there are men. However, Professor Kittredge is a great scholar. When he tells what Shakespeare meant, it is as if new sight were given to the blind. He brings back Shakespeare, the poet.

There are times when I want to sweep away half the things I am expected to learn. My mind gets too full. Sometimes, in one day, I read from four different books. They are in different languages and on different subjects. It is so confusing that I almost forget why I am reading. I am always thinking about tests and exams. My brain becomes cluttered with tiny details. Right now, my mind is full of clutter. I almost think I will never be able to put it in order.

Exams are my biggest concern. I have faced them many times and cast them down and made them bite the dust. Yet, they rise again. I feel my courage oozing out at my finger ends. I spend the days before these exams cramming my mind with names and dates. On those days, I wish that books and science and I were buried at the bottom of the sea.

At last, the hour arrives. I am lucky if I feel prepared. I try to remember the thoughts that will help me on each test. Too often, I forget. Just at the moment when I need my memory, it flies away. The facts I have gathered with such trouble simply disappear in a pinch.

I search my brain for historic facts as if I were hunting for a bit of silk in a ragbag. I am sure it is somewhere in my mind near the top. Yet, where is it now? I fish out all of the odds and ends of knowledge—revolutions, wars, and inventions. I am amazed at all the things I know that are not on the test.

Just then, the teacher says that time is up. I get a feeling of disgust. I kick the useless facts into a corner and go home. My head is full of angry plans. I wish to take away the right of teachers to ask questions without the permission of the students who have to answer them.

When Radcliffe was still in the future, it seemed romantic and wonderful. College has lost that romance. In the process, I have learned many things. I am glad that I tried the experiment. One thing I learned is how important it is to be patient. I have tried to learn to take education as I would take a walk in the country. It should be slow and open-minded.

It is said that knowledge is power. I think that knowledge is happiness. To have broad, deep knowledge is to know truth and loveliness. It is good to know the thoughts and deeds that have marked people's progress through the centuries.

So far, I have sketched the events of my life without showing how much I have depended on books. They have meant so much more in my education than they mean in the education of people who can see. I shall go back to the time when I began to read.

I read my first story in May 1887, when I was seven years old. Ever since then, I have read everything that I can get my hands on. At first, I had only a few books in raised print. They were "readers" for beginners, children's stories, and a book about the earth called *Our World*. I read those books over and over. After a while, the words became worn and pressed. It was hard for me to make them out. Sometimes, Miss Sullivan read to me. She spelled simple stories and poems into my hand. However, I enjoyed reading by myself best.

During my trip to Boston, I really began to read. I spent a part of each day in the library at the Perkins Institution. I wandered among the bookcases and took down any book I chose. Sometimes, I only understood two words on a page. Those words, however, would come back to me later when I began to talk and write. My friends were amazed at the number of words I knew. I read parts of many books until I discovered *Little Lord Fauntleroy* by Francis Hodgson Burnett. This was the first book that I really understood.

Before we began the story, Miss Sullivan explained the things she knew I would not understand. As we read, she explained the unfamiliar words. At first, there were many words I did not know. The reading was always broken up by her explanations. Pretty soon, though, I was so caught up in the story that I hardly noticed those new words. Sometimes, Miss Sullivan's fingers were too tired to go on. At those times, I felt very sorry for myself. I took the book in my hands and tried to feel the letters myself. I will never forget the longing I felt. Afterward, Mr. Anagnos had this story written in raised print. I read it again and again. I almost learned it by heart.

During the next two years, I read many books. I cannot remember what they all were, but the list includes A *Child's History of England*, as well as *The Arabian Nights*, *The Swiss Family Robinson*, *The Pilgrim's Progress*, *Robinson Crusoe*, *Little Women*, and *Heidi*.

I loved *Little Women*. It made me feel a friendship with girls and boys who could see and hear. I did not like *The Pilgrim's Progress* very much. I did not even finish it. I read La Fontaine's *Fables* in English and did not enjoy it. Later, I read the book again in French. That time I liked the style. I still did not like the stories much. I guess that I dislike stories with talking animals. They are never very interesting to me. The silly animals always seem to distract me. I seem to forget the moral of the story. However, I love *The Jungle Book* and *Wild Animals I Have Known*. I am interested in the animals in those stories because they are real animals. They are not animals pretending to be men. I understand their feelings. I laugh when they are funny. I weep when they are sad. If there is a moral in the story, I usually do not notice it.

I began to read the Bible long before I could understand it. Now, it seems that I have always known it. I remember a rainy Sunday morning when I had nothing to do. I begged my cousin to read me a story out of the Bible. She did not think

I would understand it, but she began to spell into my hand. She told me the story of Joseph and his brother. Somehow, it did not interest me. I did not like the unusual language. It made the story seem far away. I fell asleep before the story ended.

Since then, I have come to love reading the Bible. It has given me joy and inspired me. I love it more than any other book. Still, there is much in the Bible that I dislike. I am sometimes sorry that I ever read it from beginning to end. The knowledge I gained from reading it did not make up for having to read the unpleasant parts. I wish that we could somehow take out all of the ugly or cruel parts of literature without weakening the great books.

I have loved Shakespeare ever since I began reading books. *Macbeth* is the play by Shakespeare that impressed me the most. I remember every detail of the story. For a long time, the ghosts and witches found me in my dreams.

I read *King Lear* soon after reading *Macbeth*. I will never forget the horrible scene in which Gloster's eyes are put out. In the play, he is blinded as a punishment. When I read that part, I was seized with anger. My fingers refused to move. I sat still for a long moment. The blood was throbbing in my head, and I felt a huge hatred in my heart.

It seems strange that I have so many unhappy memories of my first reading of Shakespeare.

The bright, gentle plays are the ones that I like best now. When I first read them, however, I did not enjoy them.

I have read Shakespeare's plays many times. I know parts of them by heart, but I cannot tell which one I like best. My favorite depends on my mood. I like Shakespeare's poetry as much as I like his plays. I know there are many things in Shakespeare that I do not understand, but I am learning every day. I am glad when I discover new thoughts and beauty in poetry and plays.

Next to poetry, I love history. I have read many historical works. The first book that made me love history was Swinton's *World's History*. I received this book on my thirteenth birthday. Today, no one reads it anymore. I think it is wonderful anyway. From that book, I learned about how the races of man moved from land to land and built great cities. I also read in that book about how many nations encouraged art.

In college, I have read French and German literature. The German writer puts strength before beauty, and puts truth before customs or rules.

Of all the French writers I have read, I like Molière and Racine best. Also, there are parts of Balzac that feel like a fresh blast of sea air. I admire Victor Hugo, as well. His books are not my favorites, but he is a great poet, and he writes about great ideas.

I am afraid that I have written too much about my book friends. Yet, I have only mentioned my favorite authors. There are many others that I like also. However, I will not write about them all.

Books are my perfect world. In books, it does not matter if I am blind and deaf. There are no senses that shut me out from the sweet words of my books. They are not embarrassed or awkward when they talk to me. The things I have learned seem small compared to the gifts of spirit and love in books.

9 Hobbies and Interests

I hope that my readers do not think that reading is my only pleasure. I have many hobbies and interests.

More than once in my story, I have mentioned my love of the country and outdoor sports. When I was a little girl, I learned to row and swim. In the summer, when I am at Wrentham, Massachusetts, I almost live in my boat. Nothing makes me happier than to go out rowing. I take my friends when they come to visit me. Of course, I cannot guide the boat very well. Someone usually steers the boat while I row. Sometimes, however, I try to steer by the scent of water grasses and lilies on the shore. I know by the pull of the water when the oars are even. I can also tell when I am pulling against the current. It is exciting to make a boat skim lightly over waves and to feel the surge of the water!

I also enjoy canoeing. I suppose you will smile when I say that I especially like it on moonlit nights. I cannot actually see the moon climb up the sky, but I know it is there. I lie back among the pillows and put my hand in the water.

Sometimes, a little fish slips between my fingers, or a pond lily presses against my hand. Often, when we come away from the shelter of a cove, a glowing warmth flows around me. It might come from the trees that have been heated by the sun or from the water. I can never tell which.

My favorite hobby is sailing. In the summer of 1901, I visited Nova Scotia. There, I discovered the ocean in a different way. Miss Sullivan and I went to Halifax. The harbor was our paradise. We sailed past huge ships in the harbor. It was all so interesting and so beautiful!

One day we had a thrilling experience. We went out in a sailboat along with many others to watch the boats race. Hundreds of little sailboats swung to and fro close by in the calm sea. When the races were over, we turned toward home. Someone noticed a black cloud drifting in from the sea. It grew bigger and thicker and darker. Soon, it covered the whole sky. The wind rose. The waves chopped angrily. Our little boat sailed into the storm and seemed to sit on the wind. Now, it swirled in the waves. Now, it sprang up on a gigantic wave. Now, it was driven down with an angry howl and hiss. Our hearts beat fast. Our hands trembled with excitement. As the large boats and the gunboats in the harbor passed us, the seamen saluted and shouted. We were the only little sailboat out in the storm. At last, we reached home. We were cold, hungry, and tired.

I spent last summer in one of the loveliest places in New England. We were in Wrentham, Massachusetts. We stayed in the home of Mr. J. E. Chamberlin and his family. His home is called Red Farm. I remember the kindness of these dear friends and the happy days I spent with them. I played with their children, and I told them stories. Mr. Chamberlin took walks with me in the woods and taught me a great deal about trees.

I was going to write about last summer. Miss Sullivan and I left Cambridge as soon as my tests were over. We hurried to our little cottage on a lake in Wrentham. There, the long, sunny days were mine. All thoughts of work and college and the noisy city were gone. In Wrentham, we heard only a little bit about what was happening in the world. There were the beginnings of war. We heard of the fighting in the Pacific. We learned of the struggles going on among workers. We knew that somewhere, people were making history. We paid little attention to these things, as they would pass away. Here were lakes and woods and broad fields and meadows, that will last forever.

People who can see and hear are surprised that I can notice any difference between walking on city streets and on country roads. They forget that my whole body is alive to the world around me. The roar of the city strikes the nerves of my face. I feel the tramp of unseen people, and the rumbling troubles my spirit. The grinding of heavy wagons on hard streets and the clang of machines torture my nerves.

In the country, one sees only Nature's work. One does not feel sad about the struggle in city life. Several times, I have visited the narrow, dirty streets where poor people live. I become angry to think that some people live in fine houses while others live in horrible, sunless apartments. The children in these filthy alleys are hungry. They shrink from your hand as if you were going to hit them. These dear, little children haunt me with a constant pain. There are men and women, too, all bent out of shape. I have felt their hard, rough hands. I imagine what a struggle their lives must be. We think that the sun and the air are God's free gifts to all. Yet, are they? In the city's dirty alleys, the sun does not shine. The air is foul. If only these poor people could leave the city and live in the woods! If they could return to a simpler way of living! Then, their children would grow strong and healthy. Their lives would be good. I always think of these things when I return to the country after a year in the city.

What a joy it is to feel the soft earth under my feet. I can follow grassy roads that lead to brooks. I dip my fingers in the rippling water. I climb over stone walls into green fields.

Next to country walks, I like to ride on my bicycle built for two. I love to feel the wind blowing in my face and the springy motion of my bike. It gives me a delicious sense of strength. The exercise makes my pulse dance and my heart sing.

Whenever I can, I take my dog with me on a walk or ride or sail. I have had many dog friends. Right now, I have a bull terrier. He has a crooked tail and the funniest face. My dog friends seem to understand that I cannot see or hear. They keep close beside me when I am alone. I love their friendly ways and the wag of their tails.

When a rainy day keeps me indoors, I amuse myself like other girls. I read, knit, or play a game of checkers or chess with a friend. I have a special board to play these games. The squares are cut out so that the game pieces stay in place. The black checkers are flat. The white ones are curved on top. The chess pieces are two different sizes. The white pieces are larger than the black, so I have no trouble following the game. I move my hands lightly over the board to see which piece has been moved.

If I happen to be all alone, I might play a game of solitaire. I use playing cards that are marked in the

upper-right corner with a Braille symbol. Each symbol tells me the value of the card.

If there are children around, I love to play with them. I enjoy playing with even the smallest child. I am glad that children usually like me. They lead me around and show me things they are interested in. Of course, the little ones cannot spell on their fingers, but I can read their lips. Sometimes, I make a mistake and do the wrong thing. They laugh at me, and we begin all over again.

I also enjoy museums and art stores. I get real pleasure from touching great works of art. My fingertips can feel the artist's thought and emotion. I can feel hate, courage, and love in a great sculpture.

Another pleasure for me is going to the theater. I enjoy having a play described to me while it is being acted on the stage. It seems as if I were actually there in the middle of everything. I have met a few great actors and actresses. They are so talented that you forget time and place and begin to believe you are living in the past. I once touched the face and costume of Miss Ellen Terry as she played a queen. Sir Henry Irving stood beside her dressed as a king. It was a wonderful experience for me.

I remember the first time I went to the theater. It was 12 years ago. Elsie Leslie, the little actress, was in Boston. Miss Sullivan took me to see her in *The Prince and the Pauper*. I will never forget the beautiful play or the wonderful child who acted it. After the play, I was allowed to go behind the scenes. I met Elsie in her royal costume. She was a lovable child, who had golden hair that fell to her shoulders. She smiled brightly, and she was not shy or tired. I was just learning to speak at that time. I had practiced her name until I could say it perfectly. I was delighted when she understood my words. Without a thought, she put out her hand to greet me.

You can tell, then, that my life is beautiful. Everything has its wonders—even darkness and silence. I have learned to be content everywhere.

Sometimes, it is true, I feel completely alone. A cold mist comes over me as I sit alone. Beyond me, there is light and music and sweet friendship, but I cannot have it. Silence sits heavily on my soul. Then comes hope with a smile and whispers to me, "There is joy in forgetting yourself." Therefore, I try to make the light in others' eyes my sun. I make the music in others' ears my symphony. I feel the smiles on others' lips and make them my happiness.

It is not possible for me to name all the people who have made my life happy. Some of those people can be found in books. Others would be completely unknown to my readers.

I have often been asked, "Do people bore you?" I do not quite understand what that means. Of course, I do not like the calls of stupid and curious people. I especially dislike newspaper reporters. I also dislike people who think I do not understand them and talk down to me. They are like people who try to shorten their steps to match yours. Both are disturbing.

The hands of the people I meet speak clearly to me. I have met people who are empty of joy. When I grasp their frosty fingertips, I seem to be shaking hands with a snowstorm. Others have hands with sunbeams in them. Their grasps warm my heart. A hearty handshake or a friendly letter gives me real pleasure.

I have many other friends whom I have never met. In fact, often I do not have enough time to reply to all of their letters.

I am especially glad that I have been able to talk with men of genius in my life. One of these is Bishop Brooks. I have found great joy in his friendship. As a child, I loved to sit on his knee and hold his hand. Miss Sullivan would spell his beautiful words about God and heaven into my other hands. I heard him with a child's wonder and delight. He gave me a real sense of joy in life. Once, I asked him why there were so many religions. He said, "There is only one religion, Helen. It is the religion of love. You must love God with your whole heart and soul. Love every child of God as much as you can. Remember that good deeds are greater than evil deeds. If you do all this, you will have the key to Heaven." He lived out these words in his own life.

I remember the first time I saw Dr. Oliver Wendell Holmes. He had invited Miss Sullivan and me to call on him one Sunday afternoon. It was early in the spring, and I had just learned to speak. We were shown into his library. He was seated in a big armchair by an open fire. There was an odor of print and leather in the room. This smell told me that it was full of books. I stretched out my hand to find them. My fingers came upon a beautiful book of poems by Tennyson. When Miss Sullivan told me what it was, I began to recite:

Break, break, break
On thy cold gray stones, O sea!

I stopped suddenly. I felt tears on my hand. I had made Dr. Holmes weep. He asked me to recite some poems that he and I both loved. After that, I saw Dr. Holmes many times and learned to love the man as well as the poet.

I have already written of my first meeting with Dr. Alexander Graham Bell. Since then, I have spent many happy days with him. I have visited him in Washington and at his home on Cape Breton Island. I loved listening to him talk about his experiments. I also helped him to fly kites. He hopes to learn from flying these kites how to invent an airship. Dr. Bell knows about many sciences, and he can make every subject interesting. He makes you feel that if you only had a little more time, you too might be an inventor. He has a good sense of humor, and he loves children. He is happiest when he has a little deaf child in his arms. His work for deaf people will live on to help many children in the future. We love him for what he has done himself and for what he has helped others to do.

There is not enough space to mention all of my friends. Indeed, there are things about them that are too private to set down in cold print. Yet, in a thousand ways, my friends have turned my limitations into privileges. It is my friends who have made the story of my life.

I have already written of my first meeting with Dr. Alexander Graham Bell. Since then, I have spent many happy days with him. I have visited him in Washington and at his home on Cape Breton Island. I loved listening to him talk about his experiments. I also helped him to fly kites. He hopes to learn from flying them how to invent an airship. Dr. Bell knows about many sciences, and he can make every subject interesting. He makes you feel that if you only had a little more time, you too might be an inventor. He has a good sense of humor, and he loves children. He is happiest when he has a little deaf child in his arms. His work for deaf people will live on to help many children in the future. We love him for what he has done himself and for what he has helped others to do.

There is not enough space to mention all of my friends. Indeed, there are things about them that are too private to set down in cold print. Yet in a thousand ways, my friends have turned my limitations into privileges. It is my friends who have made the story of my life.

84

Selected Letters
1887–1901

Helen Keller's letters are important because they help to tell the story of her life. They are also important because they show how her thoughts and expressions grow as she becomes able to read and write and communicate with others.

These letters are remarkable because they show Keller's world as she experiences it. It is interesting to read about what speech means to her. She describes these things she "sees." However, she describes these things not as they appear to her, but as they appear to people who can see and hear. All her life, Keller tried to be "like other people."

Many of the letters included here have been shortened. Some of the words have been replaced. It is interesting to see the progress Keller showed as a child in writing and spelling. These letters were written between 1887 and 1901, the year after Keller entered college. As you read the letters, notice the words she uses. You will find that as her writing skills improve, the letters become easier to read and to understand.

After her visit to Washington, D.C., Keller wrote the following letter to Dr. Alexander Graham Bell. In addition to inventing the telephone, Dr. Bell was an expert on teaching speech to deaf people. He opened a school for training teachers of deaf people.

 TO DR. ALEXANDER GRAHAM BELL

Tuscumbia, November, 1887.

DEAR MR. BELL.

I am glad to write you a letter. Father will send you picture. I and Father and aunt did go to see you in Washington. I did play with your watch....I saw doctor in Washington. He looked at my eyes. I can read stories in my book. I can write and spell and count....I and mother and teacher will go to Boston in June. I will see little blind girls. Nancy will go with me. She is a good doll....

Good-by,

HELEN KELLER.

Keller's visit to Plymouth was in July 1888. This letter was written three months later to Mr. Morrison Heady, a blind man from Kentucky.

Mr. Heady helped to establish the American Printing House for the Blind. This letter shows how well Keller remembered her first lesson in history.

 TO MR. MORRISON HEADY

South Boston, Mass. October 1st, 1888.

...I have been in a large boat....I went to Plymouth to see many old things. I will tell you a little story about Plymouth.

Many years ago, many good people lived in England. The king did not like to have the people disobey him. The good people did not like to go to church with the king. They wanted to build little churches for themselves.

...They decided to go to a country far away. They sailed for many weeks on the deep ocean. Every day the people went upon deck to look out for land. One day there was a great shout on the ship for the people saw the land and they were full of joy because they had reached a new country safely....They were all glad when they stepped upon a huge rock. I did see the rock in Plymouth and a little ship like the Mayflower....Would you like to visit Plymouth some time and see many old things.

Now I am very tired and I will rest.

With much love and many kisses, from your little friend.

HELEN A. KELLER.

The following letter was written to Dr. Oliver Wendell Holmes, an American poet and doctor of medicine.

 TO DR. OLIVER WENDELL HOLMES

South Boston, Mass., April, 1891.

Dear Dr. Holmes:—Your beautiful words about spring have been making music in my heart, these bright April days. I love every word of "Spring" and "Spring Has Come." I think you will be glad to hear that these poems have taught me to enjoy and love the beautiful springtime, even though I cannot see the fair flowers or hear the birds singing. But when I read "Spring Has Come," lo! I am not blind any longer, for I see with your eyes and hear with your ears. Sweet Mother Nature can have no secrets from me when my poet is near....Your loving friend,

HELEN KELLER.

When Keller visited Niagara Falls, she was able to experience the distance, shape, and size of the falls. She explored the falls, crossed the bridge, and went down in the elevator. In her letter, notice such details as her feeling the rush of the water by putting her hand on the hotel window.

 ## TO MRS. KATE ADAMS KELLER

South Boston, April 13, 1893.
...I would like to tell you about the surprise that Mr. Bell and I planned for my teacher. Mr. Bell made all the arrangements before we told teacher anything about it. This was the surprise—I was to have the pleasure of taking my dear teacher to see Niagara Falls!...

The hotel we stayed in was so near the river that I could feel it rushing past by putting my hand on the window....You can never imagine how I felt when I stood at Niagara until you have had the same experience. I could hardly realize that it was water that I felt rushing and plunging with fury at my feet. It seemed as if it were some living thing rushing on to some terrible fate.... One feels helpless and overwhelmed in the presence of such a vast force. I had the same feeling when I first stood by the great ocean and felt its waves beating against the shore. I suppose you feel the same way when you gaze up to the stars at night....

Laurence Hutton was an editor of *Harper's* magazine for 12 years and a lecturer on English literature at Princeton University. The following letter was written to his wife.

 TO MRS. LAURENCE HUTTON

Wrentham, July 29, 1899.

...I passed all the tests I took in all the subjects. I even got credit in advanced Latin...But I must confess, I had a hard time on the second day of my examinations. They would not allow Teacher to read any of the papers to me. So the papers were copied for me in Braille. This worked well in the languages, but not at all well in the Mathematics. Therefore, I did not do so well as I should have done. I would have done better if Teacher had been allowed to read the Algebra and Geometry to me. But you must not think I blame anyone. Of course they did not realize how difficult they were making the examinations for me. How could they—they can see and hear. I suppose they could not understand matters from my point of view....

❖

The following letter was written to Dr. Edward Everett Hale. He was not only related to Keller, but he also was a well-known American clergyman and author. He was the grandnephew of the Revolutionary War hero Nathan Hale.

TO DR. EDWARD EVERETT HALE

Cambridge, Nov. 10, 1901.

My teacher and I expect to be present at the meeting tomorrow to celebrate the one hundredth anniversary of Dr. Howe's birth.... I am writing to tell you how delighted I am that you will speak at the meeting. I feel that you are the best person for the job. Only you can express how grateful we are who owe our education and happiness to Dr. Howe. It was he who opened the eyes of the blind and gave the dumb lip language.

Sitting here in my study, surrounded by my books, I am friends with the great and the wise. I am trying to realize how my life would have been if Dr. Howe had failed in the great task God gave him. What if he had not taken it upon himself to teach Laura Bridgman? Would I be a sophomore at Radcliffe College today? Who can say?...

Like Laura Bridgman, I have been rescued from the death-in-life existence. I know how isolated, how shrouded in darkness, how cramped and powerless a soul is without thought or faith or hope. Words cannot describe the prison-house of that darkness. Nor can they describe the joy of the soul that is released from the dark captivity. Before Dr. Howe began his work, the blind were helpless. Now they are independent and useful thanks to his great work.... Thanks to our friend and helper, our world lies upward. All of the heavens are ours!

This city was the scene of Dr. Howe's great labors and splendid victories. It is pleasant to think that we will gather to honor his noble deeds.

My teacher and I send you kind greetings....

Affectionately your friend,

HELEN KELLER.